Table of Contents

CHAPTER 1

The Changing Sky

It's early morning and the sky is changing. At dawn, the colours in the sky turn from black to purple and red.

Now the sky turns
from red to orange.
It's still dawn.

Soon the sky will
turn blue.

As the sun rises higher, it lights up the land. The water and trees start to become brighter and clearer. Daytime is coming.

It's daytime now. The sun
is high in the sky.

The sky is blue and
the clouds are white.

Now it's late afternoon and the sun has moved across the sky. It makes long shadows on the land. Day is beginning to turn to dusk.

At dusk, the sun begins to set.

The sky changes colour again.
Soon it will be night.

The sun has set. Darkness falls across the land. The sun is rising on the other side of the world. There, it is daytime. But here, it is night-time.

At night-time, the sky is full of stars. The sun is gone. Now the moon shines brightly.

YOUR TURN!

Work out what time of day each photo shows. Use the sun as a hint.

Times of Day

dawn   daytime

dusk   night-time

1

2

3

4

ANSWERS: 1. daytime;
2. dusk; 3. dawn;
4. night-time

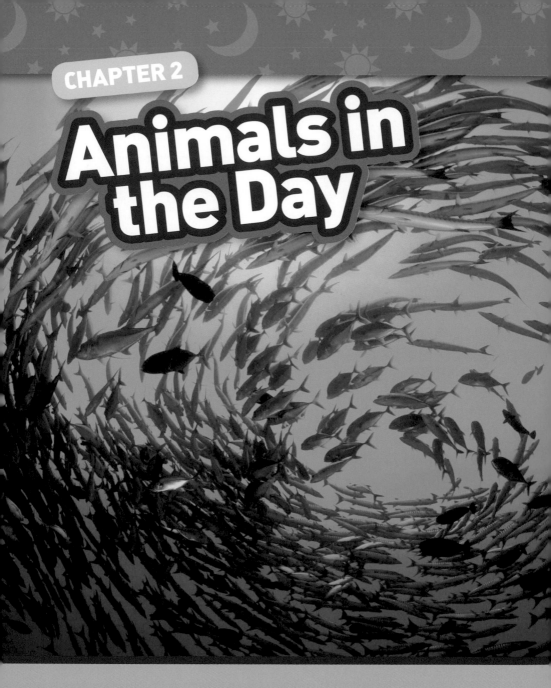

CHAPTER 2

Animals in the Day

At dawn, the sun begins to rise. Light begins to fill the water. The fish start looking for food.

The sun rises above the sea. Soon it's high in the sky and shining into the water. The fish are still moving around.

It's noon and the sun shines brightly overhead. A group of monkeys swings through the trees. The monkeys have been awake and playing since sunrise.

The sun shines on the monkeys.
It makes them warm.

The monkeys have played for
hours. Now they will take a nap.

It's late afternoon in the flat, grassy land called the savannah. The sun has started to drop. An ostrich looks out across the land.

The sun drops lower in the sky.
The sky turns orange and red.

The ostrich must eat before
the sky gets too dark.

The sun sinks lower in the sky. It's dusk. A flock of starlings comes together, like a black cloud in the sky.

The birds are safe in
the flock. They keep each
other warm.

They sing until the sun sinks
out of sight.

YOUR TURN!

What time of day does each photo show? What are the animals doing?

1

ANSWERS: 1. late afternoon, the ostrich looks for food. 2. dawn, the fish look for food. 3. dusk, the birds flock and sing. 4. noon, the monkeys play and then sleep.

CHAPTER 3

Plants in the Day

The sun shines brightly overhead. A field of sunflowers looks cheerful and yellow in the sunshine.

The flowers turn to follow the sun across the sky. This helps them collect light from the sun. They use the light to make energy.

At night, the sun does not shine. The flowers droop.

They will open again tomorrow. The sun will shine brightly again then.

It's daytime and a lotus flower opens wide. It has a strong smell and a bright colour. A dragonfly flies over to find food inside the flower.

The dragonfly needs the flower to be wide open. That way it can find food.

When night falls, the flower will close.

YOUR TURN!

Pretend to be these animals and plants during the day. Act out what each one is doing.

Run like an ostrich.

Swim like a fish.

Follow the sun like a flower.

Play like a monkey.

Fly like a bird.

CHAPTER 4

Animals in the Night

It is dark and the lions are hungry. The sun set hours ago and the only light is from the moon. The lions watch and wait.

A lion can see in the dark.

This helps it watch for food in the night.

In the dark, an elf owl peeps out of its nest in a cactus. The air is cool now and the owl can hunt. It listens for signs of prey. Soon it will set out in search of food.

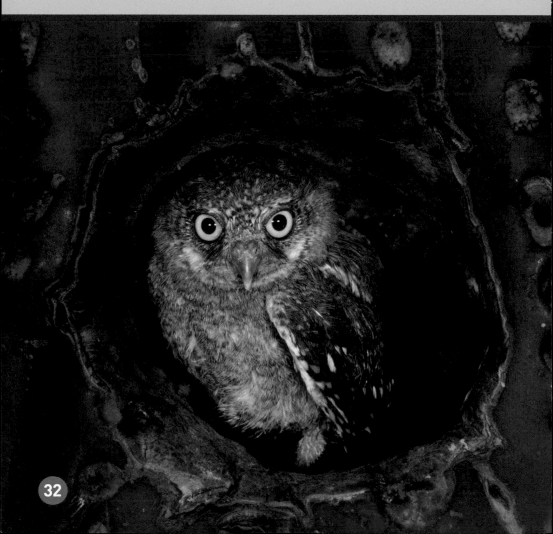

Most owls can see well at night. This owl listens, too.

It can find food even when it can't see.

In the dark, a red-eyed tree frog blinks its big eyes open. It's hungry.

The frog sits quietly and waits. Suddenly, it spots movement on a leaf.

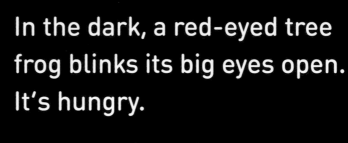

The frog is quick. It catches its food.

But it's still hungry. The frog searches for food all night.

In the dark, a raccoon wakes up. It peeps out into the night as it looks and listens. All seems safe. It's time to leave the den and hunt. The raccoon will use its excellent sight and hearing to find food in the dark.

The raccoon trots down
to the river. It peeps into
the water.

There's a fish there!

In the dark, a
termite mound
starts to glow.
It's not the
termites, though.
Hundreds of
thousands of
glowworms on
the tower are
glowing to
attract food.

The glowworms' lights shine brightly. This attracts their food.

It makes their food come right to them! Now it's easy for the glowworms to eat.

glowworm

YOUR TURN!

What sense does each animal use most to get around in the dark?
What senses do you use in the dark?

Word Bank
see   hear

1

2

3

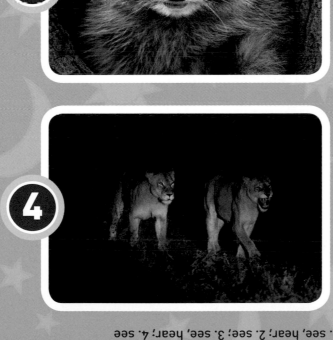

4

CHAPTER 5

Plants in the Night

Darkness falls and a balsa flower opens wide. Inside is a sweet liquid. Now, many animals can smell it. They are attracted to its scent and they come to drink.

The flower closes in the day. It will open again at night.

The nocturnal animals sleep in the day, too. They will wake up again at night.

In the dark forest,
some fungi give off a
glowing green light.

The fungi only glow at night, but they
couldn't make their light without the
daytime sunlight.

During the day, the fungi store the sun's light.

At night, they use the stored light to glow.

YOUR TURN!

Which activities do you do in the day? Which do you do at night? Tap the day side or night side of the tree as you read each activity.

sleep

see sun

see stars

see moon

swim

read

day

night

47

Published by Collins
An imprint of HarperCollins*Publishers*
The News Building
1 London Bridge Street
London
SE1 9GF

Browse the complete Collins catalogue at
www.collins.co.uk

In association with National Geographic
Partners, LLC

NATIONAL GEOGRAPHIC and the Yellow
Border Design are trademarks of the National
Geographic Society, used under license.

Second edition 2018
First published 2016

ISBN 978-0-00-831718-8

10 9 8 7 6 5 4 3

A catalogue record for this book is available
from the British Library

Printed by GPS, Slovenia

If you would like to comment on any aspect
of this book, please contact us at the above
address or online.
natgeokidsbooks.co.uk
cseducation@harpercollins.co.uk

Paper from responsible sources

Since 1888, the National Geographic Society has
funded more than 12,000 research, exploration,
and preservation projects around the world.
The Society receives funds from National
Geographic Partners, LLC, funded in part by
your purchase. A portion of the proceeds from
this book supports this vital work. To learn
more, visit http://natgeo.com/info.

Illustration Credits

*GI = Getty Images; MP = Minden; NGC = National
Geographic Creative; NPL = Nature Picture Library;
SS = Shutterstock*
COVER: LilKar/SS; (deer), Eric Isselee/SS; 1, Rolf
Nussbaumer/NPL; 2 Anton Balazh/SS; 3, iStock.
com/Brandon Alms; 4-5, Vincent Grafhorst/MP;
6, Stephen Belcher/MP; 7, Manoj Shah/GI; 8, Theo
Allofs/MP; 9, Michele Westmorland/GI; 10-11,
Michael Nichols/NGC; 12, iStock.com/Wolfgang
Filser; 13 (UP), iStock.com/GooDween 123; 13 (CTR),
iStock.com/Andreas Vitting; 13 (LO), iStock.com/
Martin Maun; 14, David Doubilet/NGC; 15, Brian J.
Skerry/NGC; 16, Yukihiro Fukuda/NPL; 17, Yukihiro
Fukuda/NPL; 18, Paul Bruins Photography/GI; 19
(LE), Vincent Grafhorst/MP; 19 (RT), Michel and
Christine Denis-Huot/MP; 20-21, Gail Johnson/
SS; 22, Paul Bruins Photography/GI; 23 (UP), Brian
J. Skerry/NGC; 23 (LO LE), Gail Johnson/SS; 23,
Yukihiro Fukuda/NPL; 24, perspectivestock/SS; 25,
Jose A. Bernat Bacete/GI; 26-27, Jane Tregelles/
Alamy ; 27 (INSET), Fotosearch Value/GI; 28 (LE),
Klein and Hubert/NPL; 28 (RT), David Doubilet/
NGC; 29 (UP), perspectivestock/SS; 29 (LO LE),
Yukihiro Fukuda/NPL; 29 (LO RT), Chris Gomersall/
Alamy Stock Photo/Alamy; 30, Frans Lanting/NGC;
31, Michael Nichols/NGC; 32, Cultura RM/Art Wolfe
Stock/GI; 33, Tom Vezo/MP; 34, Photolukacs/SS; 35,
Stephen Dalton/NPL; 36, Thomas Lazar/NPL; 37,
Rolf Nussbaumer/NPL; 38, Ary Bassous; 39, David
J. Slater/Alamy; 40, Rick and Nora Bowers/Alamy;
41 (UP), reptiles4all/SS; 41 (CTR), John Cancalosi/
NPL; 41 (LO), Brigitta Moser/GI; 42-43, Christian
Ziegler/MP; 44-45, Nick Garbutt/MP; 46 (UP LE), K.
Miri Photography/SS; 46 (UP CTR), jeka84/SS; 46
(UP RT), sripfoto/SS; 46 (LO LE), Somchai Som/SS;
46 (LO CTR), AlexRoz/SS; 46 (LO RT), studioVin/SS;
47, LilKar/SS; 47 (deer), Eric Isselee/SS